Love You

Delicious Potato Recipes for Any Occasion

BY:

SOPHIA FREEMAN

COPYRIGHTED

Liability

This publication is meant as an informational tool. The individual purchaser accepts all liability if damages occur because of following the directions or guidelines set out in this publication. The Author bears no responsibility for reparations caused by the misuse or misinterpretation of the content.

Copyright

Table of Contents

Introduction

Have you ever ordered a baked potato at a restaurant and thought that you could do a better job? Do you wish there was more you could do with potatoes other than mashed or baked? Then look no further than this simple to follow potato recipe book. Nothing is more versatile than a potato when it comes to food. You can serve potatoes as a side dish, a main course or even an appetizer. From the baked potato smothered in delicious sour cream, bacon and butter to the crispy potato French fry cooked to perfection, spuds are the perfect food when you are looking for a snack.

1.Air Fryer Crispy Potatoes

The air fryer is one of the greatest inventions for those who love frying but don't want all the grease that comes with a traditional fryer. These crispy potatoes come out hot and delicious as a snack or a side dish.

Preparation Time-5 minutes

Servings-4

Ingredients

- 16 ounces halved baby potatoes
- ½ ounce extra-virgin olive oil
- 1 teaspoon garlic powder
- 1 teaspoon Italian seasoning
- 1 teaspoon Cajun seasoning
- Kosher salt
- Freshly ground black pepper
- Lemon, cut in wedges
- Chopped parsley

Directions

1. Toss potatoes in a large mixing bowl with olive oil, garlic, Cajun and Italian seasonings. Add salt and pepper and toss to coat thoroughly.

2. Transfer coated potatoes to air fryer and cook for 10 minutes at 400 degrees Fahrenheit.

3. Splash with lemon juice and garnish with parsley.

2.Loaded slow cooker potatoes

These loaded potatoes are full of flavour after cooking slowly for 5 hours. I like to serve these with some chopped green onion, sour cream and crumbled bacon.

Preparation Time-15 minutes

Servings-6

Ingredients

- Cooking spray
- 32 ounces quartered baby potatoes
- 24 ounces Cheddar cheese, shredded
- 2 thinly sliced cloves garlic
- 8 cooked bacon pieces
- 3 ounces green onions, sliced
- ½ ounce paprika
- kosher salt
- Ground black pepper
- Sour cream

Directions

1. Using aluminum foil, line a slow-cooker and generously spray the foil lining with cooking spray.

2. Place 16 ounces of potatoes, 10 ounces of cheese, 1 sliced garlic clove, 3 pieces of cooked bacon, 1 ½ ounces of green onion and half of the paprika in the slow cooker. Season with salt and pepper.

3. Repeat the process and cover the cooker. Cook on high for 6 hours.

4. Top with the remaining of the bacon and cheese and garnish to taste.

3.Mashed potatoes

This mashed potato recipe is one of my family's favourites. The method is a little more time-consuming, but the results are delicious!

Preparation Time-25 minutes

Servings-6

Ingredients

- 4 large peeled Yukon Gold potatoes
- Kosher salt
- 6 ounces butter
- 4 ounces milk
- 4 ounces sour cream
- Ground black pepper

Directions

1. Bring some big pot of lightly salted water to a boil and add the potatoes to the pot. Cook for 18 minutes until fork tender. Drain and return potatoes to the large pot.

2. Mash potatoes until desired consistency is reached.

3. Warm butter and milk in a suitable saucepan on medium-low heat and pour over the mashed potatoes. Stir in sour cream, salt and pepper.

4. Serve with butter and garnishes.

4.Fried mashed potato balls

These tasty treats make a great potluck addition for gatherings at home or the office. I like to serve them with some sriracha mayo or sour cream for dipping.

Preparation Time-15 minutes

Servings-6

Ingredients

- 24 ounces leftover mashed potatoes
- 3 cooked slices bacon, crumbled
- 5 ½ ounces cheddar cheese, shredded
- 1 ounce chives, thinly sliced
- 1/2 teaspoon garlic powder
- Kosher salt
- Freshly ground black pepper
- 2 large beaten eggs
- 10 ½ ounces panko
- Vegetable oil

Directions

1. Mix leftover mashed potatoes in a large bowl with bacon, cheddar cheese, chives, garlic, salt and pepper until well combined.

2. Set up a dredging station by placing eggs in one shallow bowl and panko bread crumbs in another.

3. Roll balls of 1"-2" with the mashed potatoes dredge in egg and then panko. Set aside on a plate lined with parchment paper.

4. Heat 3-4 inches of oil in a large frying pan and fry the balls in the oil for 2-3 minutes per side until golden brown. Transfer each ball to a plate lined with paper towel to drain. Season with salt and pepper to taste.

5.Garlic smashed potatoes

This smashed potato recipe makes a great side dish for steak, fish or chicken. I like to serve it with a dollop of sour cream and some chives on top.

Preparation Time-25 minutes

Servings-4

Ingredients

- 16 ounces baby Yukon Gold potatoes
- 2 ounces butter, melted
- 2 minced cloves garlic
- Ground black pepper
- 1 teaspoon fresh thyme leaves
- Kosher salt
- 4 ounces fresh Parmesan, grated

Directions

1. Prepare oven to 425 degrees Fahrenheit. Put potatoes in a pot and pour in enough water to cover. Add a pinch of salt and bring water to a boil. Turn heat down slightly and simmer for 15-20 minutes until potatoes are fork tender. Unload and return potatoes to pot.

2. Arrange a rimmed baking sheet with tin foil or parchment paper and put potatoes on the sheet. Add butter, garlic and thyme and toss until potatoes are coated.

3. Press down on potatoes with the bottom of a glass and flatten into patties.

4. Sprinkle potato coins with salt, pepper and Parmesan.

5. Bake for approximately 25 minutes until crispy and golden

6.German potato salad

Serve this potato salad warm to break from traditional North American potato salad. The flavour of this dish is outstanding and your guests will devour it.

Preparation Time-15 minutes

Servings-6

Ingredients

- 32 ounces halved baby potatoes
- 6 slices bacon
- 1 finely chopped red onion
- 2 ounces apple cider vinegar
- 1 ounce water
- ½ ounce extra-virgin olive oil
- ½ ounce dijon mustard
- 1/2 teaspoon white sugar
- Kosher salt
- Freshly ground black pepper
- 8 sliced green onions

Directions

1. Apply potatoes in a pot and pour in enough water to cover. Add a pinch of salt and bring water to a boil. Decrease heat slightly and strew for 15-20 minutes until potatoes are fork tender. Unload and transfer potatoes to a large bowl.

2. Cook bacon in a frying pan for 7-8 minutes until crispy. Set aside 1 ounce of bacon drippings from pan and transfer bacon to a plate lined with paper towel.

3. Add red onion to the same pan and cook in the bacon drippings for 3 minutes. Add vinegar, oil, water, mustard and sugar. Whisk well and bring to a simmer. Remove from heat and season with salt and pepper.

4. Add green onions and stir. Pour mixture over the potatoes and toss to coat.

7.Oven fried pickled potatoes

I am a fan of pickling anything I can for that sour and addictive pickle taste. These potatoes are amazing for outdoor barbecues or family potlucks.

Preparation Time-10 minutes

Servings-8

Ingredients

- 2 thinly sliced russet potatoes
- 24 ounces pickle brine
- 1 ounce olive oil
- ½ ounce fresh dill, chopped
- 1 teaspoon garlic powder
- 1/2 teaspoon onion powder
- 1/2 teaspoon crushed red pepper flakes
- Kosher salt
- Freshly ground black pepper

Directions

1. Pour pickle brine into a large bowl and add potatoes. Add more brine to completely cover and wrap in plastic. Chill overnight.

2. Preheat oven to 400 degrees Fahrenheit.

3. Drain potatoes then pat dry with a paper towel. Transfer to a large mixing bowl and add the rest of the Ingredients. Toss potatoes until coated.

4. Arrange potatoes on some baking sheet lined with some parchment paper and place in the oven for 40 minutes. Flip halfway through to cook evenly.

5. When potatoes are crispy and golden, remove from oven.

8.Pan fried potatoes

This recipe is very simple to cook and makes the perfect side dish for any type of meat. I like to fry some potatoes when I am **Servings**teak and garlic mushrooms.

Preparation Time-5 minutes

Servings-6

Ingredients

- 16 ounces cleaned baby potatoes, sliced into ¼" coins
- ½ ounce vegetable oil
- ½ ounce extra-virgin olive oil
- ½ ounce rosemary, freshly chopped
- 1 teaspoon garlic powder
- 1/2 teaspoon chili powder
- Kosher salt
- Freshly ground black pepper

Directions

1. Heat vegetable and olive oils in a large frying pan on medium high. When oil is hot, add potatoes, rosemary, salt and pepper and cook for 4-5 minutes without touching the potatoes. They should be crispy and golden underneath.

2. Flip potatoes and cook for the same amount of time in the same way until that side is crispy.

3. Season with garlic and chili powder and cook for another 2 minutes when potatoes are fork tender.

9.Twice baked potato casserole

This potato dish is another simple potluck meal that will disappear as soon as it hits the table. Serve on the side with some sour cream on the side for extra creaminess.

Preparation Time-5 minutes

Servings-6

Ingredients

- 6 medium russet potatoes
- 2 1/2 ounces room-temperature butter
- 4 ounces room-temperature cream cheese
- 8 ounces sour cream
- 12 ounces whole milk
- 21 ½ ounces shredded cheddar cheese, divided
- Kosher salt
- Freshly ground black pepper
- 10 crumbled slices cooked bacon
- 5 sliced green onions
- 3/4 teaspoon garlic powder

Directions

1. Preheat oven to 400 degrees Fahrenheit.

2. Put potatoes on the middle oven rack and bake for 1-1 ½ hours until fork tender.

3. Take potatoes out of oven and set aside to cool for 5-10 minutes.

4. Sliced potatoes in half while still warm and scoop out flesh with a large spoon. Transfer flesh to a bowl and discard skins or use for something else.

5. Add butter, cream cheese, sour cream and milk to the potato and mash until combined. Fold 16 ounces of cheddar cheese into the mashed potatoes along with ¾ of the cooked bacon, ¾ of onion and garlic. Gradually sprinkle with salt and pepper and mix again.

6. Coat a baking dish with cooking spray or brush with butter and transfer mashed potatoes to the dish. Gradually sprinkle with the rest of the cheddar cheese and bake for 20 minutes. Remove from oven and garnish with the rest of the bacon and green onions before serving.

10.Classic baked potato

There is no such thing as the classics when it comes to offering up a delicious potato. This recipe is simple and quick and tastes amazing with some bacon, sour cream and chopped onion for garnishes.

Preparation Time-5 minutes

Servings-4

Ingredients

- 4 scrubbed russet potatoes
- Freshly ground black pepper
- Kosher salt
- Extra-virgin olive oil

Directions

1. Preheat oven to 350 degrees Fahrenheit. Poke small holes with a fork in the potatoes and rub with olive oil. Sprinkle potato with salt and pepper and bake for 1-1 ½ hours until fork tender

11.Roasted sweet potato wedges

Potatoes include the orange vegetable kind as well. These wedges are healthy and delicious when served with some Greek yogurt.

Preparation Time-15 minutes

Servings-4

Ingredients

- 3 large sweet potatoes sliced in 1/2" wedges
- 1 ounce extra-virgin olive oil
- 1 teaspoon paprika
- 1/2 teaspoon ground cumin
- Kosher salt
- Freshly ground black pepper
- 1 (5.3 ounce) container of low-fat vanilla Greek yogurt
- 1/2 large minced jalapeño
- 1 teaspoon lime zest
- ½ ounce lime juice

Directions

1. Preheat oven to 425 degrees Fahrenheit. Combine olive oil, paprika, cumin, salt and pepper and toss the sweet potatoes in the seasoning mixture until coated. Gradually sprinkle with more salt and pepper to taste.

2. Bake potatoes for 25 minutes, turning hallway through to bake evenly.

3. Mix the rest or the Ingredients in a small bowl and season with salt and pepper.

4. Serve dip with potato wedges.

12.Rosemary roasted potatoes

I like to grind the rosemary in a mortar and pestle before use so it is fine and not gritty. This dish tastes amazing with Greek yogurt and some chopped green onions.

Preparation Time-10 minutes

Servings-6

Ingredients

- 32 ounces quartered baby potatoes
- 1 ounce extra-virgin olive oil
- 4 minced cloves garlic
- 1 ounce rosemary, freshly chopped
- Fresh rosemary sprigs
- kosher salt
- Freshly ground black pepper

Directions

1. Preheat the oven to 400 degrees Fahrenheit Arrange potatoes on a baking sheet with oil, rosemary and garlic. Toss to coat and add some salt and pepper.

2. Roast for 1-1 ½ hours until fork tender.

3. Season to taste with rosemary, salt and pepper.

13.Loaded fried potatoes

If you want a healthier choice for frying, then choose some olive oil or an air-fryer for cooking. I like treating myself once in awhile by making these delectable and decadent loaded fries.

Preparation Time-20 minutes

Servings-4

Ingredients

- Vegetable oil, for frying
- 20 ounces mashed potatoes
- 4 ounces cheddar cheese, shredded
- 1 large beaten egg
- ½ ounce chives, finely chopped
- 1/2 teaspoon hot sauce
- 1/2 teaspoon kosher salt
- All-purpose flour
- Sour cream

Directions

1. Heat 2-3" of oil in a large frying pan on medium heat.

2. Combine potatoes, cheddar, egg, chopped chives, hot sauce and salt in a separate bowl and stir well. Add flour if the mixture isn't consistent enough to form balls.

3. Place balls in the oil in batches, frying for 2 minutes per side until evenly browned and crispy.

4. Serve with sour cream and extra chives

14. Antipasto salad

Make this salad for a filling main course, or a delicious side to a sandwich or fish dish. I like to serve this with some extra dressing on the side for those who like to load it on.

Preparation Time-15 minutes

Servings-6

Ingredients

- 32 ounces halved red-skinned baby potatoes
- 4 ounces chopped thinly-sliced salami
- 4 ounces cubed provolone cheese
- 4 ounces red bell pepper, diced
- 4 ounces green bell pepper, diced
- 4 ounces drained artichoke hearts, chopped
- 4 ounces sliced black olives, sliced
- 1/2 small finely chopped red onion
- 2 ounces extra-virgin olive oil
- 1 ounce red wine vinegar
- Pinch red pepper flakes
- Basil leaves

Directions

1. Bring a large pot with salted water and fully submerged potatoes to a boil and cook for approximately 8-10 minutes until potatoes are fork tender

2. Drain potatoes and cool. Transfer to a large bowl and dice.

3. In a separate bowl, whisk vinegar, oil, pepper flakes, salt and pepper until combined.

4. In a third bowl, combine salami, provolone cheese, red and green peppers, artichoke hearts, black olives and onion and mix well.

5. Mix potatoes with salami mixture then pour vinegar mixture over the salad. Toss to combine.

15. Microwave baked potato

Remember that story at the beginning of this book? I 'm not a fan of microwaving, but when you are in a hurry and want something low-maintenance, follow this simple technique for a better potato.

Preparation Time-5 minutes

Servings-1

Ingredients

- 1 large russet potato, scrubbed and pat dry with a paper towel
- Kosher salt
- Ground black pepper
- Butter

Directions

1. Poke small holes with a fork in the potato with a fork 3-4 times and place on a microwaveable plate.

2. Cook for 7 minutes on high and check to see if potato is tender. Cook in 60 second intervals until potato is easily pierced with a fork.

3. Remove potato and set aside for 2-3 minutes.

4. Cut warm potato in half and top with seasonings, butter and desired garnishes.

16. Bacon-stuffed potatoes

I'm not sure who got the idea for the first time of cheese and bacon as garnishes for potatoes, but they were a genius! Serve this with some sour cream and watch it disappear.

Preparation Time-15 minutes

Servings-4

Ingredients

- 4 large scrubbed Yukon gold potatoes
- 1 ounce extra-virgin olive oil
- 1 ounce melted butter
- ½ ounce garlic powder
- Freshly ground black pepper
- Kosher salt
- 1 teaspoon dried oregano
- 1/2 teaspoon paprika
- 6 slices bacon, cut in 2" pieces
- 8 ounces mozzarella cheese, shredded
- 2 ounces Parmesan, grated

Directions

1. Preheat oven to 425 degrees Fahrenheit. Make small cuts in the potatoes resembling an accordion. Do not cut all the way through!

2. Transfer potatoes to a baking sheet.

3. Combine olive oil, paprika, oregano, salt and pepper and whisk until combined. Brush mixture on potatoes generously.

4. Place 1 piece of bacon in each slit of the potatoes and top with both cheeses. Bake for 45 minutes until potatoes come fork tender and brush halfway through with more butter if needed.

17.Potato skin burgers

When you want to enjoy a burger without all the bread, give this fun and simple recipe a try. I like to serve these with some traditional condiments like pickles, ketchup, mustard and relish.

Preparation Time-20 minutes

Servings-4

Ingredients

- 4 Yukon gold potatoes
- kosher salt
- Freshly ground black pepper
- 1 ounce extra-virgin olive oil
- 16 ounces ground beef
- 6 slices cooked bacon, crumbled
- 12 ounces Cheddar cheese, shredded
- 4 ounces sour cream
- ½ ounce fresh chives, chopped

Directions

1. Preheat oven to 350 degrees Fahrenheit. Rub potatoes with olive oil until coated and sprinkle with salt and pepper. Transfer to a baking sheet and cook for 1-1 ½ hours until fork tender.

2. Remove potato from oven and increase temperature to 450 degrees Fahrenheit.

3. Once potatoes are cool enough to touch, cut in half along the length and scoop enough flesh out of them to leave ¼" of flesh in the skins

4. Arrange skins face down on a baking sheet and brush with olive oil. Bake for 10 minutes until golden brown.

5. Shape burger patties with the ground beef that match the size of the potato skins and transfer to another baking sheet. Gradually season with some salt and pepper and cook for 5 minutes per side until no longer pink inside.

6. Remove potato skins and fill with bacon and Cheddar. Put in the oven and bake for another 5 minutes until cheese melts.

7. Top skins with sour cream and chives and place the burger on top. Close with another potato skin or leave open-faced.

18.Grilled potatoes

When the summer barbecues come out, that is when I grill these potatoes to perfection. Serve sprinkled with oregano and extra parsley.

Preparation Time-5 minutes

Servings-4

Ingredients

- 4 large Idaho potatoes, cut into wedges
- 1 teaspoon kosher salt
- 1 teaspoon Ground black pepper
- 1 ounce garlic powder
- 4 ounces extra-virgin olive oil
- 1 ounce chopped parsley

Directions

1. Take a huge pot of salted water to boil. Add potatoes and more water if not fully submerged. Cook for 10 minutes until fork tender.

2. Drain and let potatoes cool. Preheat grill on medium high and spray with cooking spray or coat with olive oil.

3. Merge olive oil, salt, pepper and garlic in a large bowl and whisk until combined. Toss potatoes in the mixture to coat. Place potatoes on the grill for 5 minutes, turning over halfway until golden brown.

4. Add parsley to the seasoning mixture and toss potatoes again.

19.Reuben-loaded potatoes

These potatoes are a unique take on the Reuben sandwich which features sauerkraut and swiss cheese among other **Ingredients**. I love serving this potato as a delightful change of pace for lunch or dinner.

Preparation Time-10 minutes

Servings-4-6

Ingredients

- 4 medium russet potatoes, cut into wedges
- ½ ounce extra-virgin olive oil
- Kosher salt
- Ground black pepper
- 5 ½ ounces roughly chopped, thinly-sliced corned beef
- 4 ounces sauerkraut
- 16 ounces Swiss cheese, shredded
- ½ ounce parsley, freshly chopped

For Dressing:

- 6 ounces mayonnaise
- 2 ounces ketchup
- 1 teaspoon Frank's Red Hot Sauce
- 1 teaspoon Worcestershire sauce
- ½ teaspoon onion powder
- Kosher salt
- Ground black pepper

Directions

1. Preheat oven to 400 degrees Fahrenheit. Combine oil, salt and pepper in a huge bowl and toss in wedges until coated.

2. Transfer to a sheet of baking and arrange in one layer. Bake for 35-40 minutes until golden brown.

3. In another bowl, whisk all dressing Ingredients together and chill until ready to serve.

4. Remove potatoes from oven and top with corned beef, sauerkraut and Swiss.

5. Bake for another 10-12 edges are crispy around corned beef and Swiss cheese is melted.

6. Drizzle with dressing and serve.

20.Scalloped potatoes

What potato recipe book would be complete without a method for scalloped potatoes? Try these creamy treats with some extra sauce on the side or drizzled on top.

Preparation Time-15 minutes

Servings-4

Ingredients

- 32 ounces peeled Yukon Gold potatoes, sliced 1" thick
- 1 ounce melted butter
- 1 ounce olive oil
- 1 ounce fresh rosemary, chopped
- 3/4 teaspoon salt
- 1/4 teaspoon ground Pepper
- 8 ounces chicken broth, reduced-sodium
- 2 finely minced garlic cloves

Directions

1. Preheat oven to 500 degrees Fahrenheit.

2. Place sliced potatoes with oil, butter and rosemary in a large bowl. Season with salt and pepper and toss until fully coated.

3. Transfer potatoes to a metal baking dish and arrange in a single layer. Use another dish if need be, as long as potatoes are in a single layer.

4. Bake for approximately 15 minutes till golden brown and remove from heat. Flip the potatoes and bake for another 15 minutes until golden brown on the other side.

5. Remove potatoes from the oven and add broth and garlic. Bake for another 15 minutes and serve warm with extra sauce.

21.Bacon-wrapped sweet potato fries

These yummy fries are a big hit when served at kids' parties and family gatherings. I like to serve them with some sriracha mayo or Ranch dressing.

Preparation Time-10 minutes

Servings-1

Ingredients

- 3 large sweet potatoes, sliced into French fries
- 18 slices bacon
- 1/3 ounce chili powder, or more to taste
- Ground black pepper

Directions

1. Prepare oven at 400 degrees Fahrenheit. Place baking sheet with foil and set a baking rack on top.

2. Wrap each French fry with a piece of bacon and sprinkle with chili and pepper.

3. Bake for 33-35 until bacon is crispy and cooked through

4. Serve with your favourite dip.

22. Garlic butter potatoes

These potatoes taste amazing when served with a traditional meat or fish dinner. I like to add extra Parmesan and parsley to each serving for added flavour.

Preparation Time-15 minutes

Servings-8

Ingredients

- 24 ounces small potatoes
- 2 ounces melted butter
- 2 ounces extra-virgin olive oil
- 3 minced cloves garlic
- kosher salt
- Freshly ground black pepper
- 8 ounces mozzarella, shredded
- 2 ounces Parmesan, freshly grated
- 4 ounces parsley, finely chopped

Directions

1. Prepare oven at 375 degrees Fahrenheit and line a large baking sheet with parchment paper.

2. Slice slits into each potato but don't cut all the way through.

3. Transfer potatoes to baking sheet.

4. Whisk butter, oil and garlic together in a mixing bowl and brush evenly over the potatoes. Season with salt and pepper.

5. Bake for 20-22 minutes until cuts in potatoes separate.

6. Place potatoes on a large sheet pan.

7. Remove potatoes from oven, brush with more butter and top with Mozzarella and Parmesan Bake for another 23-25 minutes until crispy and fork tender.

8. Serve garnished with parsley.

23.Grilled ranch potatoes

This potato recipe packs a Ranch flavour with both seasoning and dressing in the mix. Serve drizzled with Ranch dressing and chives for added flavour.

Preparation Time-5 minutes

Servings-8

Ingredients

- 32 ounces halved baby potatoes
- ½ ounce extra-virgin olive oil
- ½ juiced lemon
- 1/2 packet ranch seasoning
- kosher salt
- Ground black pepper
- Ranch dressing
- Fresh chives, chopped

Directions

Preheat outdoor grill to Medium. Add oil, lemon juice and seasoning to a large bowl and toss potatoes in the mixture until coated.

Sprinkle with salt and pepper then thread the potatoes on bamboo skewers. Place on the grill and cook for 15 minutes until slightly charred and fork tender

Serve with ranch dressing and chives

24. Baked rosemary potatoes

This simple recipe uses a technique that sears the potato before baking to create a crispy exterior. Serve these potatoes with some extra rosemary and sour cream.

Preparation Time-10 minutes

Servings-4-6

Ingredients

- 4 large russet potatoes, pared and sliced 2" thick
- ½ ounce vegetable oil
- Freshly ground black pepper
- 1 ounce cubed butter
- 1 thinly sliced garlic clove
- kosher salt
- 8 ounces chicken broth
- 3 sprigs rosemary
- 1 teaspoon rosemary, chopped

Directions

1. Prepare oven at 450 degrees Fahrenheit

2. Sprinkle potatoes with salt and pepper. Heat oil in large oven-safe frying pan and add potatoes cut side down in the oil for 5 minutes until golden.

3. Turn potatoes over and add butter, rosemary and garlic.

4. Keep cooking for another 5 minutes then place pan in the oven. Bake for 25-30 minutes until fork tender.

5. Top with extra rosemary before serving.

25.Potato skin bites

These delectable appetizers are the perfect munchable for your next party or gathering of friends. Serve with some sour cream or sriracha mayo for dipping.

Preparation Time-30 minutes

Servings-12

Ingredients

- 3 scrubbed russet potatoes, sliced into ½-inch coins
- 1 ounce extra-virgin olive oil
- Kosher salt
- Ground black pepper
- 1 Pinch cayenne pepper
- 1 teaspoon garlic powder
- 12 ounces cheddar cheese, shredded
- 6 cooked slices bacon, crumbled
- Sour cream
- 3 thinly sliced green onions

Directions

1. Preheat oven to 400 degrees Fahrenheit.

2. Combine oil, salt, pepper, cayenne pepper and garlic and whisk until mixed well. Toss potatoes in oil mixture and transfer to a baking sheet in a single layer.

3. Bake for 30-40 minutes, turning over halfway, until fork tender and browned.

4. Remove potatoes from baking sheet and top with cheese and bacon.

5. Turn on oven broiler and broil for 2 minutes until cheese melts.

6. Serve with sour cream and green onion.

26.Breakfast volcanoes

You can watch the egg mixture bursting to the top of the potato skins in this recipe. I like to serve these with some chives and barbecue or steak sauce on the side.

Preparation Time-10 minutes

Servings-4

Ingredients

- 3 peeled russet potatoes, cut in half
- 6 slices uncooked bacon
- 5 large eggs
- 5 ½ ounces Cheddar cheese, shredded
- 1 finely chopped red bell pepper
- 1/2 finely chopped Onion
- 1 ounce finely chopped chives
- kosher salt
- Ground black pepper

Directions

1. Preheat oven to 400 degrees Fahrenheit. Line a baking sheet with parchment and set aside.

2. Scoop out the center of the potatoes with a melon baller or other small scoop until just the skin is left, no flesh.

3. Arrange potatoes cut side down on the baking sheet and wrap a piece of bacon around each one. Tuck in the ends of the bacon so they stay in place. Bake for 40-45 minutes until potato is tender and bacon is cooked and crispy.

4. In a large mixing bowl, whisk the rest of the Ingredients together except for chives and pour into each potato up to two-thirds full.

5. Put back in oven and cook for another 13-15 minutes until eggs are set.

6. Garnish with chives and season with salt and pepper to taste.

27.jalapeno popper scalloped potatoes

This recipe is another great party appetizer for the Super Bowl or Stanley Cup. I like to serve these with some savoury dipping sauces and sour cream.

Preparation Time-20 minutes

Servings-8

Ingredients

- 10 slices bacon, cut into 1-inch pieces
- 1 ounce butter, unsalted
- 3 minced garlic cloves
- 1 ½ ounces all-purpose flour
- 16 ounces heavy cream
- 8 ounces chicken broth, reduced-sodium
- 4-6 peeled russet potatoes, sliced into thin coins
- 16 ounces Cheddar cheese, shredded
- 2 thinly sliced jalapenos

Directions

1. Preheat oven to 400 degrees Fahrenheit. Cook bacon in a large frying pan on medium heat until crispy. Remove bacon, reserving ½ ounce of drippings and place on plate lined with paper towels.

2. Dissolve butter in the same frying pan and sauté garlic for 1 minute in the butter. Stir in flour and continue to stir for 1 minute.

3. Add cream, broth, salt and pepper to the flour and whisk well. Simmer for 5 minutes until mixture is thick.

4. Stir cheddar into the mixture until melted. Remove pan from heat.

5. Create a thin layer of sauce in a casserole dish and add 1 layer of potatoes. Spoon more sauce over potatoes and add bacon and jalapenos. Keep layering until dish is full. Bake for 40-50 minutes. Take off from the oven and cool for 15 minutes before serving.

28.Crock pot garlicky potatoes

Why should you do all the work when the crock pot can cook your potatoes to perfection in a few hours? These mashed potatoes taste creamy and delicious with every bite.

Preparation Time-15 minutes

Servings-8

Ingredients

- Cooking spray
- 48 ounces quartered baby potatoes
- 2 ounces butter
- 3 minced garlic cloves
- 2 ounces water
- kosher salt
- Freshly ground black pepper
- 2 ½ ounces sour cream
- 2 ounces milk
- 1 teaspoon oregano
- 1/2 teaspoon dried rosemary
- ½ ounce chives

Directions

1. Enamel the inside of a slow cooker with cooking spay. Combine potatoes, garlic, butter and water in the cooker and season with salt and pepper.

2. Stir mixture well, cover and cook for 3 hours on High until potatoes are fork tender.

3. Add milk, oregano, rosemary and sour cream to the tender potatoes and mash well. Add chives to the potatoes and serve.

29.Sour cream and onion mashed

Here is another simple recipe for mashed potatoes that tastes amazing when served with some beef and gravy. I like to make these potatoes for holiday dinners when I have the family over.

Preparation Time-15 minutes

Servings-4

Ingredients

- 32 ounces Yukon gold potatoes
- kosher salt
- 1 ounce butter
- 1 finely chopped Onion
- 8 ounces sour cream
- 4 ounces milk
- ½ ounce chives, chopped
- 1 teaspoon onion powder
- Ground black pepper

Directions

1. Cover potatoes with enough water to submerge in a large pot. Salt the water and bring to a boil. Cook potatoes for 16-18 minutes until fork tender and drain. Return potatoes to the pot.

2. Dissolve butter in a large frying pan on medium low heat. Sauté onion and salt in the butter and cook for 10-15 minutes until tender and golden brown.

3. Add onions to the potatoes and mash until desired consistency is reached. Add sour cream and milk and stir well. Serve topped with chives.

30. Twice baked broccoli cheddar

What could be better than a baked broccoli cheddar potato? One that you bake twice. Serve with some sour cream and chives.

Preparation Time-15 minutes

Servings-8

Ingredients

- 4 medium russet potatoes
- 1 ounce extra-virgin olive oil
- 1 ½ ounces melted unsalted butter
- 4 ounces sour cream
- 16 ounces grated sharp cheddar, divided
- 16 ounces finely chopped steamed broccoli
- 1/2 teaspoon onion powder
- kosher salt
- Ground black pepper
- 2 ounces warm milk

Directions

1. Preheat oven to 425 degrees Fahrenheit

2. Prick small holes into the potatoes with a fork and coat in olive oil. Place on a baking sheet and bake for 1-1 ½ hour until fork tender.

3. Remove from oven and cool for 15 minutes. When cool enough to handle, slice potatoes in half.

4. Spoon out flesh from the potatoes and place in a large bowl. Reserving half of the cheese, combine with the rest of the **Ingredients** and mash well.

5. Evenly divide filling among the potato skins and top with the other half of the cheddar. Bake until the cheese is melted for 15 minutes.

Conclusion

Whether you are throwing your potatoes into an air-fryer or frying them up in a skillet, be confident that one of these recipes will suit all your potato needs. When you are planning the menu for your next holiday gathering or trying to change up the family dinner, give one of these simple dishes a try. You will be glad you did!

About the Author

A native of Albuquerque, New Mexico, Sophia Freeman found her calling in the culinary arts when she enrolled at the Sante Fe School of Cooking. Freeman decided to take a year after graduation and travel around Europe, sampling the cuisine from small bistros and family owned restaurants from Italy to Portugal. Her bubbly personality and inquisitive nature made her popular with the locals in the villages and when she finished her trip and came home, she had made friends for life in the places she had visited. She also came home with a deeper understanding of European cuisine.

Freeman went to work at one of Albuquerque's 5-star restaurants as a sous-chef and soon worked her way up to head chef. The restaurant began to feature Freeman's original dishes as specials on the menu and soon after, she began to write e-books with her recipes. Sophia's dishes mix local flavours with European inspiration making them irresistible to the diners in her restaurant and the online community.

Freeman's experience in Europe didn't just teach her new ways of cooking, but also unique methods of presentation. Using rich sauces, crisp vegetables and meat cooked to perfection, she creates a stunning display as well as a delectable dish. She has won many local awards for her cuisine and she continues to delight her diners with her culinary masterpieces.

Author's Afterthoughts

I want to convey my big thanks to all of my readers who have taken the time to read my book. Readers like you make my work so rewarding and I cherish each and every one of you.

Grateful cannot describe how I feel when I know that someone has chosen my work over all of the choices available online. I hope you enjoyed the book as much as I enjoyed writing it.

Feedback from my readers is how I grow and learn as a chef and an author. Please take the time to let me know your thoughts by leaving a review on Amazon so I and your fellow readers can learn from your experience.

My deepest thanks,

Sophia Freeman

https://sophia.subscribemenow.com/

Printed in Great Britain
by Amazon